HORSE TALES

GW00507312

Harry Sear

Illustrated by

Michael Avery

© Harry Sear 2008
Horse Tales

ISBN 978-0-9560128-0-7

Published by Harlin House Publishers
Charity Farm
Eggington
Leighton Buzzard
Bedfordshire LU7 9PB

A CIP catalogue record of this book
can be obtained from the British Library.

Book designed by Michael Walsh at
THE BETTER BOOK COMPANY

A division of
RPM Print & Design
2-3 Spur Road
Chichester
West Sussex
PO19 8PR

CONTENTS

150 years in 2010

R·A·B·I

Supporting Farming Families

As a tribute to the farming community and the farming folk who have told many of these tales, twenty-five pence from each copy of *Horse Tales* sold will be donated to the **Royal Agricultural Benevolent Institution** who with compassion and discretion provide welfare advice, care and financial provision to those in the farming community suffering need, hardship or distress. R.A.B.I can be contacted on tel 01865 724931 or www.rabi.org.uk.

Thanks to Pollinger Ltd. for permision to use an extract from
H.E. Bates 'The Vanished World'

INTRODUCTION

I have collected these 'Horse Tales' over the last twenty years and sadly many of the tale tellers have passed on. I thank the people, from all around the country, who recounted tales either from their own experience or from memories told to them. In shining a light onto our past they light our way into the future.

Many thanks also to Michael Avery for his brilliant illustrations.

The age of the working horse came swiftly to an end after the Second World War. Luckily, memories and tales of that bygone age are more durable than smelted horse ploughs, decayed wagons or rotted harness.

Most of the tales are of a light hearted nature, some are clearly jokes, some have the clear ring of truth, some need to be taken with a pinch of salt. But isn't it often the seasoned dish which is the tastiest?

Harry Sear
Eggington
Bedfordshire
2008

Foreword By Edward Kelsey
~ Joe Grundy in 'The Archers'

I am sure Joe Grundy would be as flattered as I am to be invited to write the foreword to this delightful little book. He would remember when most farm implements were powered by men or horses and given half a chance would regale you with tales of ploughing matches which he really should have won had not an Archer tricked him out of it. And although those days are long past he continues to demonstrate his equine skills with his smart little pony and trap. He treats Bartleby, his pony, as one of the family and is never happier than when driving him at a gentle trot along the country lanes of Borsetshire.

I am old enough to remember when horses were not only used on farms but, apart from the ice-cream man on his tricycle and the butcher's boy on his bike, all deliveries were made using horse-drawn vehicles. The baker and the grocer with their vans, the milkman and the coalman with their carts and of course, Joe would remind me, the brewer's dray drawn by a splendid pair whose breed reminds him of his favourite tipple – a pint or (if you are paying) a quart of the "Bull's" famous "Shires". Oh, the nostalgia! This little book took me back to my childhood, listening wide-eyed to the tales my mother told of her favourite uncle's pair of shires; the time they bolted or the day they refused to cross the ford; how sometimes, as a special treat, she was allowed to sit atop them with their brasses jingling and flashing in the sun – which in those days was always shining.

Edward Kelsey
Guildford June 2008

THE BEGINNING AND THE END

The earliest evidence of domestication of the horse was the excavation, in Central Asia, of the ceremonial burial site of a warlord, buried complete with his chariot and two galloping horses in harness. So for at least 6500 years the horse was man's most important means of motive power, carrying armies to war, transporting people, hauling loads and tilling the land.

This long and crucial role came to a relatively sudden end, as the Industrial Revolution got into full swing around 1830 and the ring of the blacksmith's hammer was overtaken by the thud of steam hammers and the din from Victorian engineering works. The first commercially successful steam traction engine, which could out pull a team of horses, was rolled out by Ransomes of Peterborough in 1840.

However, competition for both steam traction engine and the horse was not far behind, as the internal combustion engine was developed; the first automobile production being started by the German, Karl Benz in 1888.

So swift was the takeover from the horse that, soon after the end of the Second World War, the internal combustion engine had almost completed its takeover. The influence of the horse on our way of life had all but ceased.

Childhood Memories

As for myself I was born in 1948, on a 500 acre mixed farm in the village of Eggington in South Bedfordshire and have my own childhood memories of the last three horses my father kept. These being a pair of Suffolk Punch mares, Blossom and Sally, and a medium weight black pony called Molly, who was used to pull a float for all light fetching and carrying jobs. The heaviest work was already being done with tractors and the heavy horses left the farm in the mid 50s. The pony and float stayed on until George Orchard, the horseman for forty years, retired.

I have vivid memories of regular outings with George, to "do the foddering" the float piled high with bales of hay and bags of chaff mixed with black treacle and chopped mangels to feed the cattle outlying in the fields around the parish. The thrill of being allowed to take charge of the worn leather reins and guide the pony along one of the dry ridges of a ridge and furrow pasture field, while George threw wads of hay from the back of the float to the hungry cattle who jostled for position behind.

But George and the pony left the farm before the 1960's were born. The float and the two big tumbrel carts were parked in a corner of the farmyard to crumble away. The flat wagon served as a platform for the milk churns until the change-over to tanker collection. Most of the horse-drawn implements lay amongst the nettles, until finally sold to the scrap man. The last working horse in the area was used on the Co-op milk round in the neighbouring town of Leighton Buzzard until the late Sixties. This truly was the 'tail end' of the working horse era.

A float is mentioned in several of the tales so it would be as well to describe its construction. It was a single axle cart, with sides around three feet high, it's area was around four foot by six and it had a tail board which let down with chain supports so that it could extend the floor area if necessary. A removable plank from side to side served as a seat and this could be adjusted forwards or backwards to get the float balanced, for the comfort of the pony. Originally with wooden wheels, by the time I knew them most had been converted to pneumatic tyres, often by replacing the axle with one from a scrapped automobile. I suppose the float was the horse age equivalent of the pick-up truck.

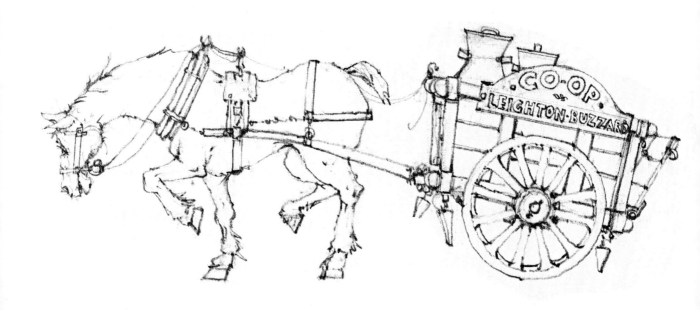

"He pulled the lastest milk float in the west"

TALES FROM MANOR FARM EGGINGTON BEDFORDSHIRE

Sleeping on the job

My Father had a new steel dutch-barn built around 1934. The barn was 90 feet long by 40 feet deep and 18 feet to the eaves: quite a sight in those days. The steel components came by rail, from Mains Ltd of Glasgow, to Stanbridge Ford Station on the Leighton Buzzard to Dunstable branch line. Load upon load of steel were fetched by horse transport the two miles to Manor Farm.

On one particularly warm afternoon a waggoner was sent, with an old horse and two wheeled tumbrel cart, to fetch some of the steel. The cart was, somewhat imprudently, loaded with some of the longest girders, which were balanced on top of the high sides, projecting forward over the horse and back over the rear of the cart. The driver perched himself on the front corner of the cart with his feet resting on the shafts. The precarious load set off at a walk back to the farm. The driver began to nod off in the heat and the horse wearily plodded homewards on auto-pilot.

The horse turned left opposite Stanbridge church into Eggington Road and began to heave its load up the hill towards Eggington. As they reached the steepest part of the hill the girders slid backwards on the cart, which tipped the cart up, the shafts lifting the bemused horse clear of the ground.

Luckily the girders dug into the road behind, preventing the cart rolling back. And that is how a search party from the farm found the situation a while later. The horse, fast asleep, hanging in the shafts and the driver sleeping on the cart, both blissfully unaware!

"Sleeping on the job"

Fire Down Below

Many horses have a common character trait of stubbornness — if they decide they're not going to do something then its hell's own job to make them. Methods of coaxing would often be unconventional.

My grandfather, whom sadly I never knew, was also called Harry Sear. I'm told that he could be an impatient man. One day he visited the harvest field to see how work was progressing and found the horse and wagon loaded with sheaves, standing in the middle of the field with the farmhands gathered round. Asking what was going on, they told him that despite all their coaxing, tugging, pushing, slapping and shouting, the horse wouldn't move. Grandfather had his own idea on tactics. He grabbed a sheaf of corn, put it under the horse and set it alight. Unfortunately the horse proved to have either a martyr's nature or a particularly high pain threshold, for he still refused to budge and the fire was hastily put out before any serious damage was done. On being unhitched from the wagon, the horse immediately walked on, its strike protest for a rest period successfully concluded. Grandfather's technique might have seemed cruel, but as some mitigation, can I say that similar stories were sent to me from others; though their horses all moved on a bit smartish!

"Burnt at the Cart"

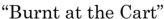

Home Alone

Another tale from Eggington concerning a stubborn horse tells how Ray Jenkins, a worker at Manor Farm, was driving a pony and float up Nursery Lane to get back home for his mid-day meal. Realising that it was getting late he tried to get the pony to break into a trot, but, as it wasn't the pony's dinner that was getting spoiled, the nag refused to be hurried.

Now Ray had his shotgun with him in the float, so he fired off both barrels a few inches behind the horse's ear. This immediately had the desired effect, the shocked horse launched itself forward achieving the equine equivalent of nought to sixty in six seconds and was soon over the brow of the hill and galloping into the village ... Unfortunately Ray Jenkins was still standing in the float in Nursery Lane ... The old harness had broken with the sudden snatch of acceleration, the shafts had dropped to the ground and the horse galloped off by itself.

Home Alone

MORE TALES FROM BEDFORDSHIRE AND AROUND THE COUNTRY

Sting in the tail

A tale of more horse turbo-charging was recounted by George Kingham from Tilsworth, Beds. As a boy-chap (too old for boy and not old enough for chap) George had worked for Bunkers of Trinity Hall Farm, Hockliffe. One day he was riding as a passenger in the float, back to the farm, after a visit to the market in Leighton Buzzard.

Now Market Days in Leighton Buzzard were known as Tiddly Tuesdays, because the pubs were open all day, so the farmhand that George was with had taken the opportunity for an early drink or two, which meant they were late getting back to work.

Anyhow, when they got out of town onto the open road the farmhand decided the pony wasn't putting enough effort into speeding them along, so he leant over the side of the float and with his horny hand plucked a bunch of stinging nettles from the roadside, lifted the pony's tail and wedged the nettles underneath. The more the nettles stung, the harder the pony clamped its tail down, and the harder the pony clamped its tail down, the more the nettles stung, and the more the nettles stung, the faster the pony went.

"By God, you should have seen us go," said George. "We overtook the bus afore we got to Hockliffe!"

"Hope you've got a dock leaf!"

Battle of Wills

Another tale from George Kingham was of a horse with a considerably less sluggish nature in fact this one had a definite wild streak.

Before the Second World War it was common for farms to grow mangel-wurzels, a large sweet watery beet, which were used as cattle feed in the winter. The curious name, by the way, comes from the beet's German origins, mangel meaning beet, and wurzel meaning root. Mangels were dug up in the late autumn and put in clamps, long narrow heaps, covered with straw and soil to preserve them and keep them from freezing.

In the winter the mangels were put through an agricultural version of a food processor, which on my Father's farm went by the wonderful name of the Mangel Grittler. This would slice up the mangels into large chips. These we would mix with chaff or chopped straw and thick black treacle to feed the cattle.

Anyhow I digress. George, working at Trinity Hall Farm, alongside the Watling Street on the Dunstable side of Hockliffe, was sent with a tumbrel cart, to a field on the other side of Hockliffe to pick up a load of mangels and bring them back to the farm for clamping. Now most horses could be relied upon to stand still unattended whilst the cart was being loaded, even to move on or stop at command. Not this animal: it fidgeted the whole time, stamping and snorting, throwing its head around and chewing on its bit. A farmhand had to hold the horse's head the whole time, making more work for the others loading the cart.

The field they were in had a slope away from the road and the ground was soft going, so to 'larn the beggar a lesson' the horse and cart were taken down to the bottom of the field and the cart was piled up high above its usual limits.

George got up on the front of the cart, onto that usual precarious perch, with his feet on the narrow strip at the corner of the shafts and his bottom on the edge of the cart and took the reins. The horse's head was let go and off they went up the field towards the road. The theory was, that with the extra weight and the steel banded wheels cutting deep into the soft ground, the horse would be exhausted by the time it reached the road and would have 'larnt some manners'. Not so, the horse seemed to relish its task and pulled and pulled until in quick time they were at the road. There was no indication that the horse was tired out or had learnt any manners. Indeed it seemed intent on teaching its driver a thing or two.

Once on the road, it was downhill into Hockliffe. The horse resisted any attempt that George made to rein it in and broke into a full gallop. George was reduced to clinging on for dear life as the uneven motion of the gallop made the cart buck up and down. They charged down the Watling Street through Hockliffe, George shouting "whoa", together with a few other words that would have made a trooper blush. The horse's hooves rattled on the road like machine gun fire, with the steel-banded wheels rumbling like thunder. George recalled "We turned a few heads and there were mangels flying everywhere!"

The runaway continued breakneck, home to Trinity Hall Farm, nearly tipping the whole lot over as it turned sharply into the farm drive, finally coming to a halt in the farmyard. The horse sweating a bit but still fidgety and full of life. On hearing what had happened

"Whoa!"

the foreman ordered the horse to be harnessed to the heaviest roll they had and set it, with George in charge, to roll the pasture field next to the farm.

It still took several hours of lugging the heavy roll before the horse showed any signs of exhaustion. Although only sat on the cast iron seat mounted above the centre of the roll, George said he was on his last legs long before the horse. I asked if the horse had 'larnt' its lesson. No said George, "A few days later it was uppity as ever, it never did larn any manners."

The Final Furlong

Not all horses had that sort of energy. A tale came from Lancashire of an incident around the end of World War Two. A farmer employed a farm worker aged 78. The old chap was set to work with an equally ancient horse (in horse years), chain-harrowing a pasture field, with the old fellow walking alongside leading the horse.

The farmer and his family were just sitting down to lunch when the old man came hobbling into the farmyard, no horse in sight. The farmer leaned out of the window and asked the old fellow what was wrong. The old fellow replied, "Master, I've walked the bugger to death!" The old horse had collapsed and died at work.

"I've walked the bugger to death!"

A Grave Tale

Wherever there is life there is death. A tale came from Mrs C.E. Rodgers of Pentre-Beirdd, Near Welshpool. One of the farm horses died and the farmer ordered two farm hands to bury it while he went to Oswestry Market. He told them where to dig the hole and to fetch one of the shires from the field to drag the corpse into its grave – not the float pony as the corpse was too heavy for him to pull.

The men sweated all morning digging a great hole. They looked at the shire a long way away in the field and at the float pony nearby in the orchard and decided 'what the governor couldn't see he wouldn't grieve about', so they fetched the pony.

The pony managed to pull the dead horse along side the hole, the men unhitched the chain, took the pony round the other side of the hole and refastened the chain, but when they asked the pony to pull, disaster struck: the pony took a step backwards as he felt the weight and fell backwards and upside down into the hole where he became firmly wedged.

The farmer returned to find the men frantically digging to release the pony.

"I think we are safer in here with the horse."

You've Been Framed

Drunkenness featured in many of the tales that I have been told. A common practical joke, it seems, was played by young lads on well-known heavy drinkers, who had their horses tethered up outside an Inn. This involved taking a horse out of the shafts of whatever it was pulling and putting it back in between the shafts the other way round, so it was facing the cart. The boys would then hide and wait for the entertainment when the owner returned, the antics being more amusing in proportion to how squiffy the owner was!

An instance of this was sent from Driffield in Yorkshire. A man remembered that when he and his brother were lads on the farm, an old scrap dealer called Charlie, a friend of their father, would visit and their father and Charlie would sit drinking for hours in the farm kitchen. For devilment, one such visit, the boys turned the horse round in the shafts and waited. When Charlie weaved his way out of the farmhouse he stood and surveyed the scene, scratching his head in a rather fuddled bemusement. Then deciding that action needed to be taken he went to the cart and got his ash stick which he waved in the horses face, " Well you beggar, you've managed to kick the cart over your head, now you can bloody well kick it back again!"

A common variation on this was if there was a convenient five-bar gate, the jokers would unharness the horse, put the shafts of the cart through the gate and put the horse back in the shafts on the other side of the gate. If the owner was drunk enough he would heave himself up into the cart and try to drive off, bemused as to why the horse wouldn't move on.

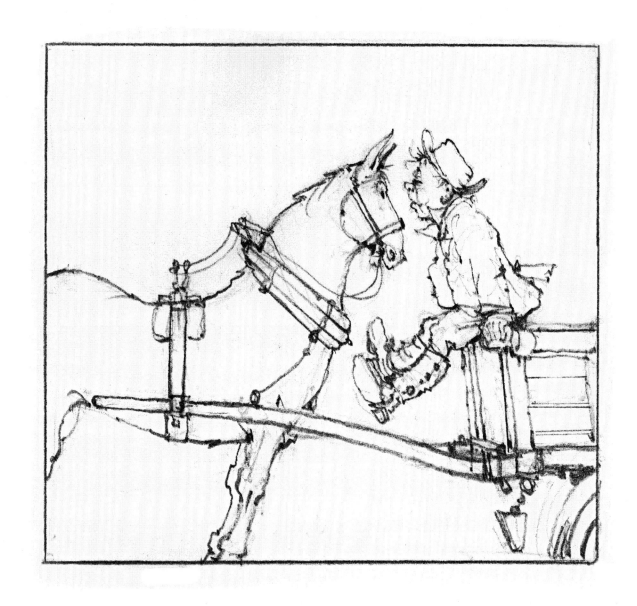

"You've been framed!"

Identity Crisis

There are many tales of people getting drunk and being placed in a stupor in the bottom of their carts and the horse set loose to pull its owner home, or horses getting loose and going home on their own. This often came to grief, when the horse, without the guidance of a driver, got the wheel of the cart caught round a gatepost or other obstacle, or the horse tried to get through the stable door to get its feed whilst still harnessed to the cart.

A joke on this theme came from Mr Mills of Bude, Cornwall, and was told to him as a boy of fifteen in 1935. Farmer Giles decided he would take a few pigs to sell at 'Tavy' (Tavistock Market in Devon) so he put the 'hoss' in the float, loaded the pigs and set off. The pigs sold well and farmer Giles went to the Tavern for a jar or two of cider. An hour or so later and a bit tiddly he got into the cart and set the 'hoss' looking towards home and promptly fell asleep in the bottom of the float. The old 'hoss' was well used to the journey and was plodding on happily without help from his master, when a pal of the farmer came along and decided to play a trick on his friend. He stopped the 'hoss' took it out of the shafts and sent it on home leaving Farmer Giles asleep. When Farmer Giles woke up he got onto his knees, raised his head above the sides of the float, looked about himself and said "Well, if I be Farmer Giles I've lost my hoss. If I bain't be Farmer Giles I've found me a cart."

Creatures of habit

Many incidents came about because the horse is a creature of habit. Whilst this ability to learn routines could often be useful, it also had its disadvantages.

John Kerr, a blacksmith from Leighton Buzzard remembered that as a lad he worked with Tom Tift, a blacksmith in Linslade. They used to regularly ride out to do work for Lord Rosebery on the Mentmore Estate some three miles away across the Buckinghamshire border. Their transport was Tom's lightweight four wheeled flat wagon, which had shallow sides and a seat across the front. Now it was their habit, on the way home, to call in for a drink at the 'Hare and Hounds' at Ledburn and when they got there, the Landlord at the pub would always give them a large arrowroot biscuit for the horse.

One evening they were running late and Tom, in a hurry, wanted to get straight back to Linslade. They were trotting along at a fair old clip and Tom had only a light touch on the reins. As they reached the 'Hare and Hounds' the horse thought they were going to call in for their usual refreshment and without slackening in pace, turned sharp left into the pub forecourt, nearly upsetting the cart. Taken by surprise, John and Tom were thrown sideways off of their perch, landing in a heap on the grass verge. I don't think the horse got its biscuit on that occasion.

'A turn for the horse'.

Variations on a theme

I have been told that the ability of a horse to put regular routes into its auto pilot memory was always a risk for unfaithful husbands, as they might be found out by a suspicious wife, who would ride her husband's horse with the reins slack so that the horse would lead her to her rival's door. If you had a mistress, it was safer to walk!

A lady in Leighton Buzzard told my wife that her father would get her to lead his horse to the blacksmith on her way to school. The blacksmith would shoe the horse then turn it loose, slap it on the rump and it would go home itself.

It wasn't always the horse that found its way home by itself. Joan Alcock of Eggington remembers her great-uncle Harry Edwards getting rather forgetful in his old age and going to Leighton Buzzard in his pony and trap, but forgetting how he got there and coming back home on the bus. When he got back to collect his pony, he found the horse had got so fed up it had lain down at the side of the road in the shafts.

"Fed up"

Bread to the oven

W.T. Pollard told me that as a lad he worked for a baker in Kent. The baker had bought a new horse, from a dealer, to pull the delivery van. One day they were on the delivery round, young Pollard and the baker had gone, with their baskets of bread, down the garden path and round to the back door of the house and had stopped talking to the housewife. When they went back to the road, the horse and bread van was nowhere to be seen.

It turned out that the baker's horse had been waiting patiently in the street, when a horse drawn hearse and funeral procession had come by. The baker's horse, pulling the bread van, had fallen in behind the procession and followed it several miles from Maidstone to the crematorium just outside Bearstead. The baker later learned that the horse's previous owner had been an undertaker and it was just doing what it had been used to in its previous working life.

Not so well bred

Talking of bread vans, Mr Brantom, who owned a seed merchants in Leighton Buzzard, told me of Len Deeley who drove a baker's van and was heading towards Hockliffe Road when his horse took fright and began to gallop out of control, with Len hanging on for dear life. A lady who needed some bread put her hand out crying shrilly "Baker! Baker! Len always the soul of politeness managed to tip his hat and shout "Sorry Ma'am – Can't stop – I'll do you on the way back!"

Another tale concerning a baker, was of the horse used to deliver bread in the Kingswood and Rowington area of Warwickshire. On alternate weeks his owner rode this same horse to hounds. If ever the hunt happened to come into the district on delivery days the bread boy couldn't do a thing with him and had to lead the horse home and do the whole round on his bicycle, which meant making many journeys. Obviously the horse, much like its owner, preferred going hunting to working.

"I'll do you on the way back!"

The Vanished World

Now let us put all these rose tinted memories into perspective. Another description of a baker and his horse is given by the famous author H. E. Bates, in chapter seven of his brilliantly evocative autobiography, 'The Vanished World' :– 'The baker, a thin, rather ill looking, cadaverous man, always appeared to be saturated with ghost-like clouds of whiteness. In the little yard outside the bakery his horse and bakers cart were stabled. A pile of saddened dung always steamed on the air, the ammonia sting of it powerful enough to kill even the aroma of the bakery. On winter nights a weary looking horse and an even wearier looking baker came home at walking pace, journeying home, the golden candle flames in the cart lamps flabbily flickering in the dark air'.

This grim realism is also recalled in Chapter Two, as H. E. Bates talks of his grandfather's smallholding –

'A succession of horses, some of them no more than ponies, inhabited the stables. One by one with disconcerting frequency they fell down dead. Since their unremitting task was to draw, plough, harrow, seed drill, horse hoe, trap and truck from which we sold vegetables fruit and flowers from house to house two mornings a week, this was not surprising. It is in fact astounding that the tumbrel from the knacker's yard did not appear more frequently than it did to take away its melancholy load of stiffening horse flesh.'

"Not all sleek shires"

The black and white horse

A practical joke was recounted by B. Banwell of Chilcompton, near Bath. This concerned a relative of their father, who every Sunday, would ride his large black mare to a village some eight miles away in order to court his lady love. On arriving at the village he would stable his horse at the Inn and walk the few yards to the home of his beloved.

One of these nights a few of the local lads decided to play a trick on the visitor to their parish. They got a brush and a bucket of whitewash and whitewashed the black mare from head to hoof. Much later that night, the lover came to get his steed and finding only a pure white horse in the gloom of the stable he came to the conclusion that his own horse had been stolen and this white horse must belong to a late arrival at the Inn. Embarrassed, as the hour was far from respectable, he thought it prudent not to wake anybody and so walked the eight miles home, only finding the truth of the matter when he walked back the next day!

"You've missed a bit in the corner".

Call-up papers

An instance of a horse being painted, in rather different circumstances to the last tale, comes from B.D. Oliver of Hayle in Cornwall. This occurred during the 1914-1918 war, when the Government was requisitioning horses from the farms to send to the army. Mr Oliver's grandfather was told to get all his horses gathered together as a Government Agent was coming to pick out the horses that were to be taken. Now amongst the farmer's horses was an old black mare that he didn't mind being taken off the farm. His best horse was a bay mare, a lot younger but a similar build to the old mare. So the young bay mare was dyed black and the old mare was hidden on another farm. When the Requisitioning Officer came to see the horses and pick what he wanted it was obvious he would pick the best, and one of those was the bay horse dyed black. Just what the farmer wanted!

The officer gave the farmer a list of the horses that he wanted and the date to take them to the railway station for transport to the Army. At the station another official had the description of the horses that were to be delivered to him and was quite satisfied when a seventeen-hand black bay mare was presented.

Back on the farm the young mare was washed to her original colour and put back to her work and all parties were satisfied … "You see good horses were hard to get then."

"I'm too old"

Sacrifice

The First World War had a devastating effect on the working horse population of Britain. There were over one and a half million horses employed in the theatre of war and British horse casualties numbered over half a million.

For centuries Britain's horse breeders had been selectively breeding to improve the quality of working horses. The practice of the Government to requisition the best horses for the War Effort had a far reaching effect on the quality of horses in the country. It was an added factor in the demise of the working horse, speeding the inevitable change to the combustion engine as motive power.

"We remember"

Military Matters

Horses had been used in the theatre of war for centuries. The cavalry being at the sharp end of land warfare.

Gough Michael from Stanbridge, Bedfordshire, told me the tale which was said to be about the Seventeenth and Twenty First Lancers, 'The Death or Glory Regiment'. A cavalry instructor was drilling a team of six horsemen. They were ordered to go out to a point away from the instructor then trot back past him and draw their swords swiftly on the command "draw". They then had to repeat this exercise at the gallop.

When it came to repeat the exercise at the gallop the instructor bellowed out: "And we don't want no more bloody one eared 'orses!"

Kept in the dark

Gough Michael was fond of a joke and here are a couple concerning horses as well as harking back to a bygone age.

In the coal mines in the 1930s, the miners were given a docket which told them their pay and any deductions. One day one of the pit ponies went berserk, running full tilt along the tunnel past the overman and out of the pit. The overman recognised the pony and which ostler was supposed to be looking after it. He asked the man what the hell was going on. The ostler said he didn't know what was wrong; all he had done was to show the pony his pay docket.

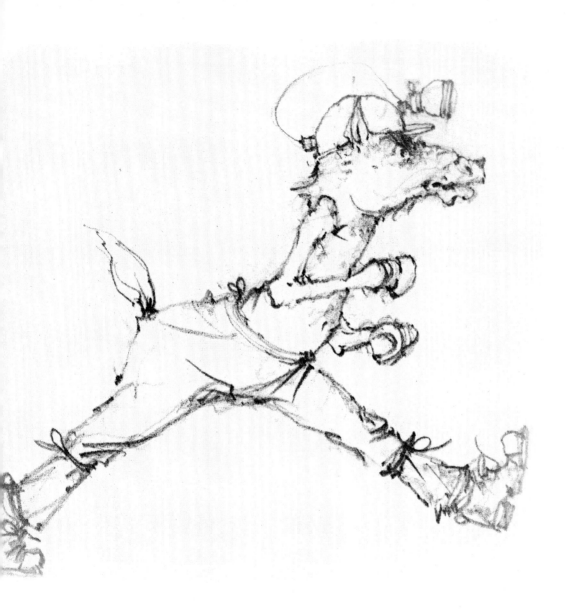

'If you pay peanuts ...'

Not Cricket

A horse was playing cricket, the bowler bowled and the horse hit the ball a good crack, quite enough for an easy single. But the horse didn't run. When asked why he didn't run the horse replied, "Blimey, if my owner knew I could run, he'd have me in the two-thirty at Ascot!"

"If my owner knew I could run!"

Tales of the Unexpected

Because horses have a mind of their own many of the tales come about because of the animal's unpredictability.

George Kingham told of the day that the first Belisha beacon was put at the crossing on Hockliffe road outside the Dolphin public house. A farmer calling in for a drink thought the beacon's post ideal for tethering his horse to. Whilst he was in the pub something startled his horse, causing the animal to pull back on the post, which was not yet properly set in the ground. The post fell over, breaking the beacon and the horse towed it quite a way down the road.

Unfortunately the police station is only yards from the Dolphin and the matter came to the notice of the local Constabulary. George said that no charges were laid, but the farmer had to give the policeman a chicken and a dozen eggs … "That's how it was in those days."

Marked for Life

Blacksmiths John Kerr and Tom Tift used to shoe the three big dray horses that were kept by the Railway Company at the stables in Linslade station yard. The shed used as the shoeing shed was a timber-framed and boarded building. There were metal rings in the end wall to tether the horses while they were being shod. John had got a red hot shoe out of the fire and put it on the anvil which had some water on it. When red hot metal is put on a wet anvil it causes an explosive crack and one of the horses took fright and pulled back. The whole end of the building started to move and the shed threatened to collapse.

John saw disaster coming and froze, but old Tom moved like lightning and picked up the red hot shoe with the pricket (the tool used to present hot shoes to the horses hoof) and pushed it onto the horse's rump, the shock making the nag jump forwards, thus saving the day. The branding effect of the red hot shoe meant that for years the dray horse was seen around Leighton with a perfectly white, horse-shoe mark on its rump.

"Where can I get one done like that?"

Fosset's Elephants

A unique tale came from Philip Hiskin of Snitterfield, Warwickshire. The local milkman drew up to the Nags Head in Hockley Heath, with his horse and milk float, for his usual lunchtime drink. His horse was standing patiently outside, when who should come trundling and trumpeting along the road but the two elephants from Fosset's Circus, being moved to their winter quarters.

The horse took one look at the strange creatures and bolted towards home. The milkman gave chase on foot and the customers at the pub alerted the local policeman who set off in pursuit, on his bicycle, blowing his whistle and shouting "whoa!" Eventually they all finished up outside the door of the horse's stable.

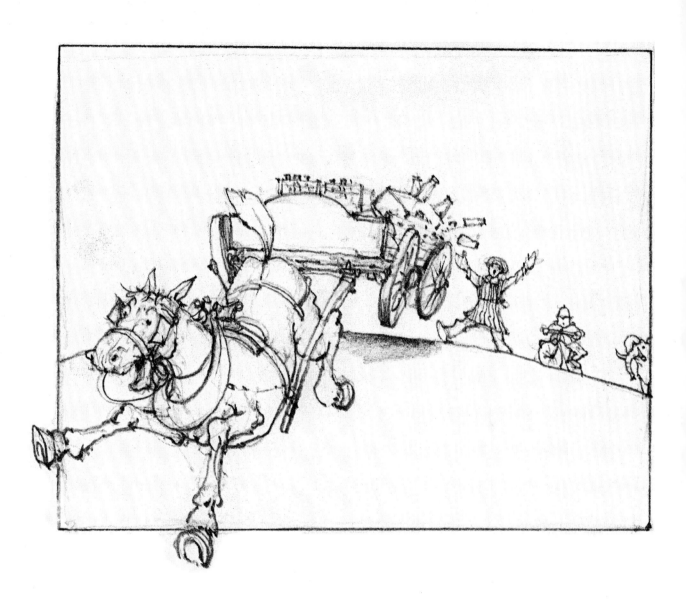

'Took one look and bolted'.

The City Tale

Most of our tales so far have been from the more rural parts of Britain however, research reveals that the history of horse transport in London in the Nineteenth Century was quite a story in itself.

London in the 1840's had a horse population of over a quarter of a million horses. The streets were teeming with horse-drawn trams and coaches, carriages, vans, carts, tumbrels, gigs, broughams, phaetons, floats, dogcarts, donkey carts, wagons, tilburys, landaus and drays etc. etc, together with twenty thousand single horse riders, tens of thousands of pedestrians as well as herds and flocks of animals going to various London markets. (Incidentally, Arthur Ingram's book *Horse Drawn Vehicles since 1760*, lists 325 different types.)

The congestion became so acute that in 1845 a Royal Commission was set up to try and find a solution and from that came a proposal by Charles Pearson, the surveyor to the City, for an underground passenger railway system. This suggestion was met with great opposition. The Duke of Wellington warned that, "One day a

French army will arrive in London before we even know they have landed in England!

But the chaos in the streets continued and in 1863 the first section of the Metropolitan Underground Line was opened between Paddington and Farringdon Street in the City. It was a filthy and primitive set-up to start with; the passengers sitting on bench seats on open wagons exposed to the soot and smoke from the steam locomotives, but it was so readily accepted by the population that on its first day thirty thousand passengers were carried and the development of the London Underground System was assured.

The Underground took some trade away from horse transport in London, but of course the main competitor was to be the steam engine, quickly followed by the internal combustion engine and 1904 saw the first petrol engine cabs in London. The meter to estimate the fare was called a taximeter and so we got the name taxicab. There were 8000 'taxis' in London by the First World War but the horse-drawn cab didn't die out immediately; in 1927 there were still just over a hundred horse cabs, the last one leaving the streets in 1947.

Move over, Darling

The number of horses in a crowded urban environment meant that horses were sometimes stabled in unexpected places. The luxury of mews stabling was not available to everyone:

A memory was shared with me by Mrs Field, an elderly member of the Eggington WI who had been brought up living in a terraced town street. A few doors along from her house lived a coalman and his family. It was neither safe nor possible to stable his horse at his coal-yard and so it was kept in the small back-yard of his house. Nothing so unusual about that, you may be thinking. The only thing was, the only access to the back-yard was through the house and every morning and evening the furniture had to be moved out of the way for the coalman's dray horse to be let through the kitchen and parlour.

The coalman's wife often complained about this but was told that was the way they made their living and it was not up for discussion.

"Move over …"

Slippin' and slidin'

Twenty five years or more ago we used to have big hessian bags of dried sugar-beet pulp delivered to the farm to mix into the dairy cows' feed. This pulp was the dried residue left after the sugary juice had been pressed from the sugar beets at the factory.

The load on one particular day was being delivered by a haulier called Timberlake who came from Markyate, Hertfordshire, 25 miles from London. The younger Timberlake was being helped that day by his father who although around his eighties was handling the bags like a good 'un.

Timberlake senior told us that he had been in haulage since a lad, apart from a period which he served in the First World War. He had just started his working life at the start of that war, as a young helper to a waggoner, hauling loads of fodder into London for the resident horse population and often hauling loads of horse manure back out of London, to be used as fertilizer on the farms.

The flood of able-bodied men joining the Army had caused a labour shortage and one day his boss came to him and said that the waggoner had left and the then fifteen year old Timberlake would have to take the next day's load of hay into London by himself.

At dawn he set off with a two horse team and a heavy load of hay. He knew the way and he was good with horses so things were going fairly well; he got into London but when they reached a steepish hill the load started to push the horses and their hooves started to slip and slide on the shiny cobbles. At this time the waggoner would put his weight on the lever that pressed the wooden brake blocks against the steel-rimmed wagon wheels to take the pressure off the horses. Young Timberlake applied the brakes with all his might but he was not strong enough for his efforts to have any effect. I can remember the elderly Timberlake's words to this day: "Them 'orses, they slipped and slid down that hill faster and faster, I thought they'd go over any moment. I was scared out of my wits. Well I weren't going to do that again, so next day I went to the nearest recruiting office, lied about my age and joined the Army".

The sugar beet was unloaded and it is to my regret I never met the gentleman again, as I bet he had a few more tales to tell.

White horse in

Another tale of horses being taken indoors comes from Buckinghamshire. In the late 18th and early 19th century there used to be a great steeple chase held at Aylesbury in Buckinghamshire, with a lot of allied festivities. Like the big horse-racing events of today, these occasions were attended by all the 'nobs'. One year the Marquis of Waterford was holding court at the main inn, of the day, which was the 'White Hart'. After having had quite a bit to drink the Marquis decided to have his horse fed at one of the tables in the dining room. The horse was bought in and all went well, the horse eating its oats from a bowl on the table. The trouble arose when they tried to back the horse away from the table. The horse slipped on the wooden floor, panicked and went completely berserk, smashing much of the furniture, crockery, glassware and windows.

The next year, 1851, again at The Steeple Chase Stewards' Dinner, a young buck took a bet to do the same. This young man went one better as he rode his small white pony into and around the dining room, where he took another bet that he could jump his pony over the banqueting table. This he did, but getting over-confident he tried it again, but this time the pony's hoof caught in the table cloth pulling food, wine, glasses, cutlery and crockery to the floor. The young man, not having the same credentials or wealth as the Marquis of Waterford, was banished from the function, but the little pony remained famous for its exploit and when sold years later made well above its value on the strength of it.

'There's a horse in my soup!'

Speeding Carr

Another tale of horses being ridden into hostelries is the story told by J. A. Carr who was born at Castle Donnington. He recounted that his father at the age of three rode his pony up the steps of The Moira Arms Hotel, in the front entrance, through the hotel and out of the back door.

He also tells that when his father was adult he rode his horse the 22 miles to and from Castle Donnington to Leicester five times in one week to be a Juror on the 'Green Bicycle' murder case. One night in a particular hurry he rode the 22 miles in one hour and five minutes.

I was particularly interested in this last story as I had been told that my grandfather, Harry Sear, owned a very light trap and a fast pony and that he would trot from Eggington to market in Bedford, some 18 miles, in around an hour. Mr Carr's letter gives that some validity.

By the way, the same journey by car today can still take up to an hour, taking into account the traffic congestion.

Is that progress?

"Do you mind if I stand?"

Horse Traders

Before the days of the second-hand car salesmen there were horse traders and they had much the same reputation. A tale concerning them came from Philip Hiskin of Snitterfield. This tells of the parson who wanted to change his old horse for a younger one, so he rode over to the Stow-on-the-Wold Horse Fair with his horse and gig. He parked the gig and unharnessed the horse and had soon sold his old horse for ten pounds and started looking round for a new one. After a couple of hours, down the street came trotting a beautiful cob, all clipped out, ears pricked up, his tail gingered under and flowing in the wind. Just the type of horse the parson liked.

The parson decided to buy the cob, he paid seventeen pounds ten shillings and another shilling for a new halter. He harnessed him up and headed for home. He was very pleased with his new horse with its ears pricked up, trotting excitedly along – very similar in many ways to his old horse.

When he got home he unharnessed his new horse in the yard. The horse pulled free and trotted straight across the yard round the end of the stable and into the paddock then immediately over to the corner with the water trough. Only then did it dawn on the parson that he had bought his old horse back from 'The Horse Copers of Stow'.

"Sid's second hand nags"

Buyer Beware

Buying a horse was always something of a risky business as it was always difficult to assess the faults and foibles of any particular animal on first sight. This is illustrated by the tale told by John Dick, of Morpeth, Northumberland.

A man was very keen to buy a particular horse from a horse dealer. The dealer said that the horse had only two faults, "I will tell you one now and the other after you buy him. The first fault is that he is a bad catcher." "Oh that's no problem," replied the buyer, who really liked the look of this horse and the reasonable price. "I have a small field which funnels down to the stable so I can easily run him in." So the purchaser handed over the money. "Now what is the other fault?" He asked. The dealer replied, "He's no bloody good when you have caught him!"

From the Heart

John Dick also sent me a long, eloquent and evocative account of his experiences of a life working with horses. "I have been a farm worker all my life, still working part-time at sixty eight. I have always loved heavy horses and worked with them until taking over the tractor. I hung up the reins for the last time in 1960". (This was written in 1988.)

I have driven all kinds of heavy horses in my time and found you got the most out of them treating them with kindness ... On larger farms the first horseman always came out of the stable first, followed by the second horseman and so on, the lad with the odd horse came last and there was trouble if anyone stepped out of place. The first horseman also had to loose first when working in the fields. Most men took a great pride in their horses and would put them before themselves. If they could, they would get into the granary and steal a bit of linseed cake; this put a good shiny skin on them, or a bit of fishmeal kept them in fettle.

I remember one day passing an old man on the road. He said, "You have been at the linseed cake," as I had a black horse whose coat was

... been at the linseed cake

shining. Most farmers didn't mind as it showed you had an interest in your horses. I heard of a man who, when asked if he would stay for another year, said he would if he could have a new brime [Scottish word for collar] for his black mare. That was more important to him than money.

When the horses were being replaced by tractors there was great rivalry between the horsemen and the tractormen ... When I was ploughing or working on the land with horses the old boss used to come and see how I was getting on but when another lad was working along side me with the tractor he lost interest as the standard of work dropped.

As the horses were being replaced, many horsemen took over the tractors and I know some who used to talk to them the same as they did to the horses. Many fences were knocked down as a tractor wouldn't stop when given a word of command!

I had once a horse that I could drive without reins. I once went to scuffle turnips with him and forgot the reins; I worked all morning with him, just by talking to him.

When I first started to drive a pair of horses their names were Punch and Matt. When they got pensioned off they spent their time in a field being fed hay outside in the winter.

A neighbour who had a small holding with not much work thought they would do for him, so the boss and I decided to let him have them for nothing, as we knew they would be well off, but he killed them with kindness. He put them in the stable and the good feeding was too much for them. Punch was found dead one morning. A few days later Matt took bad, he was down in the field and couldn't get up. The farmer and I made him comfortable with some straw and I took a bit of hair from his mane, which I still have, because I knew it would be the last time I saw him. He was 22 years old and Punch slightly younger.

When Punch was eight years old he went deaf which made him difficult to work with. The vet said he might drop dead anytime but after a few weeks he got his hearing back and lived another 13 years. He was a steady-going horse, who pulled the same whether it was empty or loaded with a ton …

We had a horse called Charlie who wasn't castrated until he was six years old. He could open the sneck of the gate with his neck and used to get out and graze the farmyard which had a green. He would also walk down the road to our neighbour's croft and go in his farmyard and graze it. Everyone knew Charlie and his tricks. If we didn't want him to get out we used to put a stone between the sneck.

Great Fosson was a heavy place for horses to work. When carting down the steep bank it was easier for the horse to hold back the cart if they could get one wheel off the road into the side, but this made a mess of the road and you were in trouble with the roadman who took great pride in the length of road allotted to him."

John Dick's letter ended with a dialect poem, about the uneasy transition from horses to tractors:

The horseman was a man

But times hae changed and tractors noo
hae taen the place o' the horse,
But there's nothing like so picturesque
As the ploo'ins rode and course.
For what could beat a weel matched pair
Turned oot a spic and span.
While a tractors driven by a loon
The horseman was a man.

When one door closes another opens

The passing of the horse age was not mourned so greatly by all. Blacksmiths, who shod horses, had a job that was backbreaking and often dangerous and many of them realised that there was a lucrative and less arduous future for them in the new motor age. They learned the skills of motor car repair and turned their premises into garages.

In 1911 one such blacksmith, Stan Merritt, wrote some lines as a parody of Longfellow's 'The Village Blacksmith':-

> Beneath a huge electric sign,
> The village smith now sits;
> His brawny form, though plump and fat,
> His easy chair just fits.

> The old clay pipe is laid away,
> His brow reveals no sweat;
> He calmly views the cars roll up
> And puffs a cigarette.

Six shining pumps adorn the spot
Where once the anvil stood;
The heavy traffic daily pays
This modern Robin Hood.

Well, at least it's a job".

How wrong can you be

Some horse users at the start of the twentieth century were slow to realise how the motor age would affect their lives. The editor of a trade paper in 1903 wrote this:-

'According to reports from all parts of the country the motor craze is bearing its fruit in bringing the machine into contempt. Contempt is scarcely the word – most people are simply disgusted with the craze. The novelty will soon wear off, like the brilliancy of tinsel or cheap jewellery. And it will be relegated to the limbo of exploded fads.'

Three years later an American journal commented on whether the car would ever replace the horse:-

'I cannot see it and think that those who look at it in that way are short-sighted. Twenty years from now the junk dealers will be buying all the old automobiles for scrap. It will be just like the bicycles – going out about as quickly. The man who believes that the automobile is going to supplant the horse in his use is to my mind completely in the dark'.

How wrong they were!

ANY MORE FOR ANY MORE?

This collection only skims the surface of recollection and anecdote of the horse age that must exist. If you have any memories, quotations, stories or recollections from your own experience or recounted to you, or, if you know someone who might have such memories, get them to pass them on. I would be pleased to read them and consider them for 'Horse Tales Two'.

Likewise I am collecting tales about any aspect or subject, town or country, from the world that is constantly vanishing into the mists of time – to see more clearly where we are going it helps to know where we have come from.

All communications will be acknowledged. Wishing you all peace and good health.

Harry Sear
Charity Farm
Eggington
Leighton Buzzard
Beds. LU7 9PB.

harry@sear7743.freeserve.co.uk